Kingfisher Books, Grisewood & Dempsey Ltd
Elsley House, 24–30 Great Titchfield Street
London W1P 7AD

First published in 1988 by Kingfisher Books

BRITISH CATALOGUING IN PUBLICATION DATA
Rice, Melanie
   All about our world
   1. Environment – For children
   I. Title II. Rice, Chris III. Smith, Leslie
   333.7
ISBN: 0 86272 332 9

Edited by Vanessa Clarke
Editorial assistant: Camilla Hallinan
Designed by Ben White
Cover designed by Pinpoint Design Company
Colour separations by Scantrans Pte Ltd, Singapore
Phototypeset by Southern Positives and Negatives
(SPAN), Lingfield, Surrey
Printed in Spain

MELANIE & CHRIS RICE

ALL ABOUT OUR WORLD

Illustrated by
Lesley Smith

Kingfisher Books

Contents

Our world

From far out in space our world
looks something like this.

You can see the clouds
swirling over the land and
sea beneath.

We all live in the same world but each of us sees it differently, depending on where we live.

dry deserts

cold mountains

hot rain forests

crowded cities

seasides

flat river valleys

9

Mountains

People who live high in the
mountains do not have many
visitors. Fierce winds and snow
often make their homes difficult
to reach.

A quarry

Rocks and stones cut from the lower slopes of mountains and hills are used to build . . .

. . . dams . . .

. . . churches . . .

. . . temples . . .   . . . and statues.

Volcanoes

A volcano is formed when red-hot rock from deep inside the earth breaks through the hard outer crust.

For hundreds of years some volcanoes seem to be sleeping.

When a volcano erupts, hot ash and lava spurt out. The rivers of lava burn everything in their path. The lava becomes hard when it cools.

Forests

Different kinds of forests grow in different parts of the world.

▶ Coniferous forests are found on mountain slopes and in other cold places. The trees grow cones and long, pointed leaves.

◀ Rain forests grow where it is always hot and wet. Many brightly coloured animals live among the rich green leaves.

▶ Deciduous forests grow in cooler places. Almost all deciduous trees lose their leaves in winter and grow them again in the spring.

Trees provide food and shelter for many animals. Can you see where these animals live?

red deer

gorilla

woodpecker

puma

grey parrot

Tree-felling

People cut down trees when they need . . .

. . . land to build homes and grow crops on . . .

. . . and wood to make things with.

It is important to plant new trees because tree leaves help to keep the air clean and tree roots hold the soil in place. Without trees, land can turn into deserts of dust.

Hot places

Deserts form where there is little or no rain. They are bare and empty because most plants and animals cannot live there.

An oasis is a place in the desert where water can be found. Naturally, people build villages around oases.

Oil in the desert

Big pools of oil are hidden deep beneath the sand and rocks of some deserts.

plastic

cloth

Things made from oil

petrol

Camels

Camels can travel for days without food in the desert because they store fat in the humps on their backs.

Plants and animals able to live in the rocky desert of North America

lizard

cactus

kangaroo rat

snake

Cold places

Large parts of our world are covered with snow and ice for most of the year. Yet people still live there. These people are living in the Arctic.

In winter some Arctic hunters build igloos to sleep in. Igloos are made from blocks of ice but they are warm inside.

These animals live around the North Pole in the Arctic.

polar bear   **ringed seal**

arctic hare   **snowy owl**

Herding reindeer for food in the Arctic

These animals live around the South Pole in the Antarctic.

Weddell seal

emperor penguin

whale

Living in the city

People live in cities all over the world.

Can you see where they live and work and where they go to enjoy themselves?

Cars, buses, bikes, taxis and underground trains all help people to move quickly from place to place.

18

Building in the city

Many people work together to build houses and flats. Architects draw up designs to show how the new flats should be built. Workers clear the building site and dig out the foundations.

Bricklayers build walls of bricks and mortar. They spread the mortar with a trowel.

Carpenters make the doors and window frames and fit the floorboards.

Tilers fit tiles to the wooden roof frame. The tiles help to keep out bad weather.

Plumbers put in the water pipes and gas pipes. They make sure there are no leaks.

Electricians lay the wires that carry electricity to the wall sockets and lights.

Plasterers and painters finish the walls before people move into their new home.

People at work

All over the city people are working. Here are some of the jobs they do. You can see where some of these people work on pages 18–19.

computer operator

secretary

car worker

shopkeeper

van driver

road sweeper

policeman

road mender

22

firefighter

nurse

doctor

teacher

hairdresser

chef

bank clerk

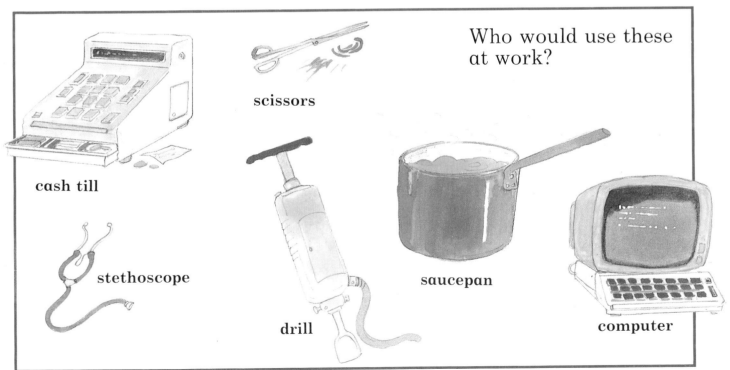

cash till

scissors

Who would use these at work?

stethoscope

drill

saucepan

computer

On the farm

The farmer's job is to grow food.
Milk, meat, eggs, vegetables and
fruit are all produced on this farm

Can you find?

goose

hen

pig

cow

sheep

duck

sheepdog

A food chain

Corn soaks up energy from the sun and ripens.

A hen gets its energy from eating corn.

We get our energy from eating the hen's eggs.

This is called a food chain.

The ranch

A farmer on a ranch keeps herds of cattle. Some ranches are so large that the farmer travels around by helicopter. The ranch-hands use horses and jeeps on the grassy plains.

The sheep station

Large flocks of sheep are grazed on grasslands. Every year they are rounded up and their wool is sheared.

Lambing is a busy time on sheep farms. Sometimes lambs have to be fed milk from a bottle.

The fleeces of wool are sent to market, then on to mills to be spun into knitting wool and threads for making cloth.

Growing food

Farmers grow food in every part of the world.

Harvesting bananas from trees in Surinam

Harvesting rice from plants in China

Cutting down sugar-cane in Jamaica

Collecting apples from an orchard in France

Picking groundnuts from bushes in Gambia

28

Harvesting tomatoes
in a greenhouse in
Belgium

Picking tea-leaves from
bushes in Sri Lanka

Cutting cocoa pods from
trees in Ghana

Growing wheat

First the farmer ploughs the earth
and sows wheat seeds.

Rain and sunshine make the seeds
grow. The sun ripens the grain on
the plants.

Finally the farmer cuts the ripe
wheat with a combine harvester
and harvests the grain.

Water all around

Wherever we live we need water. This village has grown up near a river. Its people can use the river to water their fields and to travel on. A well provides fresh drinking water.

Can you find?

a well for drinking water

a barge which carries goods

a water-wheel which raises water

children swimming

Water in our taps

reservoir

pump

cleaning filter

The water in our homes comes from rivers and reservoirs. It passes through a filter which cleans it.

Then it is pumped to us along pipes. We use the water for drinking, cooking and cleaning.

The story of a river

High in the mountains, rain and melting snow form streams which join together and flow down to the sea as a river.

In the hills the river flows along quickly. It falls over rocky cliffs as waterfalls.

snow

waterfall

reservoir

dam

lake

A lake forms when the path of a river is blocked.

Lakes that are made by building dams are called reservoirs.

As it nears the sea, the river becomes deeper and flows more slowly.

32

rain

river mouth

The place where the
river meets the sea is
called the river mouth.

A river mouth where the tides
flow in and out twice a day
is called an estuary.

At the seaside

The seas hold most of the world's water. Some people go to the seaside on holiday but others live and work there.

The wind from the sea is strong. Can you see what it is blowing?

Tides
The sea rises and falls twice a day – at high tide and low tide.

low tide   high tide

Fishing

Fishermen sail into the harbour to unload the fish they have caught in their nets. On the quay people buy some of the fish. The rest is packed in ice to keep it fresh, and taken to market.

SILLY SALLY

A seafood chain

Tiny plants called plankton live in the sea.

Small shellfish eat the plankton. Then larger fish eat the shellfish.

We are at the end of the food chain and eat the bigger fish.

plankton → **shellfish** → **fish** → **fish and chips**

Without plankton, we would have no fish to eat.

Markets

Markets are places where people buy and sell things. There are many different kinds of market.

A flower market
in the Netherlands

A fruit and vegetable
market in Bolivia

A fish market
in Japan

A clothes market
in Nigeria

A spice market
in India

A pottery market in Tunisia

To market

Food and other goods are sent to markets nearby but they are also sent to markets in countries far away.

Can you find out where your food comes from by looking at the labels on tins and packets?

A supermarket which sells many different things under one roof

Clothes we wear

We wear clothes to keep us warm . . .   . . . to keep us cool . . .

. . . to keep us dry . . .   . . . and to protect us at work.

We wear special clothes for special occasions.

We wear special
clothes . . .

. . . for sport . . .

. . . to show people who we are . . .

. . . and just for fun!

What are clothes made from?

The material for our clothes
comes from plants and animals
and from factory-made threads.

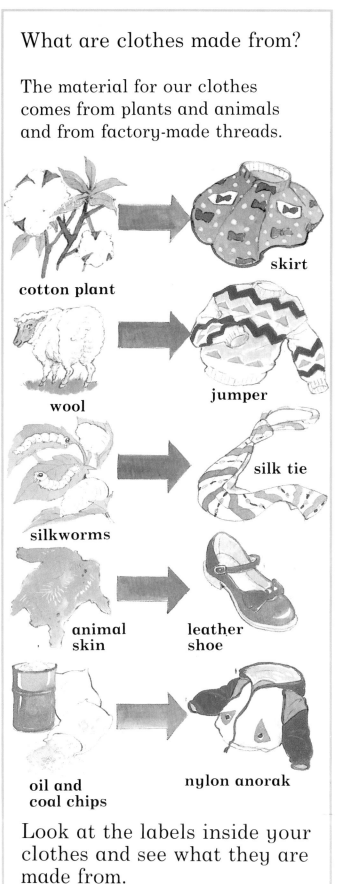

cotton plant

skirt

wool

jumper

silkworms

silk tie

animal
skin

leather
shoe

oil and
coal chips

nylon anorak

Look at the labels inside your
clothes and see what they are
made from.

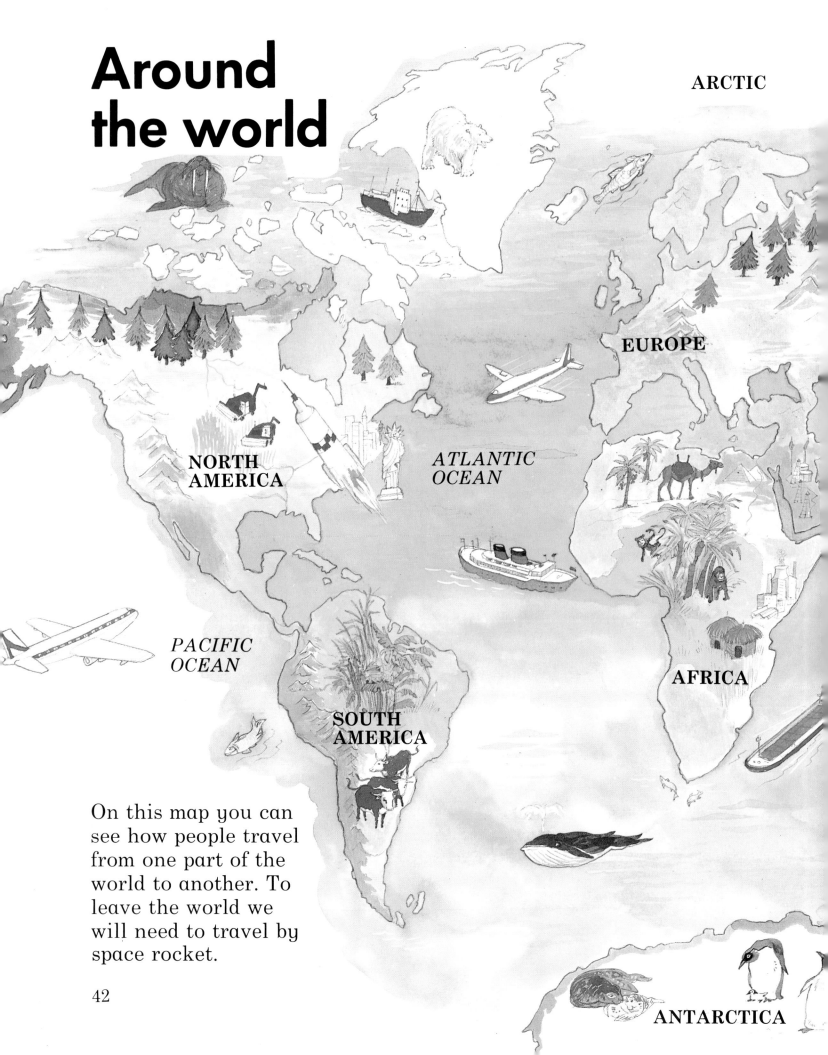

Around the world

ARCTIC

EUROPE

NORTH AMERICA

ATLANTIC OCEAN

PACIFIC OCEAN

SOUTH AMERICA

AFRICA

On this map you can see how people travel from one part of the world to another. To leave the world we will need to travel by space rocket.

42

ANTARCTICA

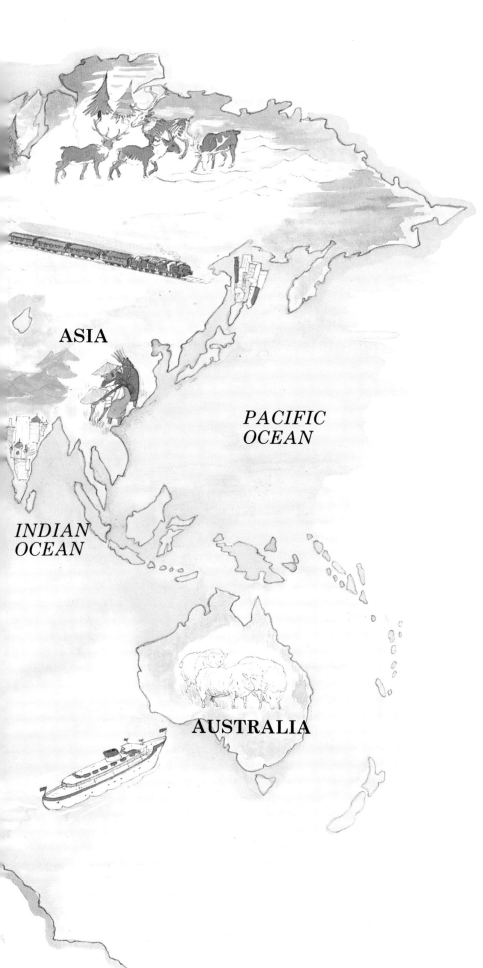

ASIA

PACIFIC
OCEAN

INDIAN
OCEAN

AUSTRALIA

Can you find?

aeroplane

ship

space
rocket

oil
rig

train

camel

polar bear

Finding out

We can find out more about our world by visiting other countries . . .

. . . listening to stories from other lands . . .

. . . looking at postcards and photographs . . .

. . . reading books and magazines . . .

. . . listening to the radio and watching television.

Index